SHAKIRA

A Real-Life Reader Biography

Wayne Wilson

Mitchell Lane Publishers, Inc.
P.O. Box 619
Bear, Delaware 19701

First Printing

Real-Life Reader Biographies

Paula Abdul	Mary Joe Fernandez	Ricky Martin	Arnold Schwarzenegger
Christina Aguilera	Andres Galarraga	Mark McGwire	Selena
Marc Anthony	Sarah Michelle Gellar	Alyssa Milano	Dr. Seuss
Drew Barrymore	Jeff Gordon	Mandy Moore	**Shakira**
Brandy	Mia Hamm	Chuck Norris	Alicia Silverstone
Garth Brooks	Melissa Joan Hart	Tommy Nuñez	Jessica Simpson
Kobe Bryant	Salma Hayek	Rosie O'Donnell	Sinbad
Sandra Bullock	Jennifer Love Hewitt	Rafael Palmeiro	Jimmy Smits
Mariah Carey	Hollywood Hogan	Gary Paulsen	Sammy Sosa
Cesar Chavez	Katie Holmes	Freddie Prinze, Jr.	Britney Spears
Christopher Paul Curtis	Enrique Iglesias	Julia Roberts	Sheryl Swoopes
Roald Dahl	Derek Jeter	Robert Rodriguez	Shania Twain
Oscar De La Hoya	Steve Jobs	J.K. Rowling	Liv Tyler
Trent Dimas	Michelle Kwan	Keri Russell	Robin Williams
Celine Dion	Bruce Lee	Winona Ryder	Vanessa Williams
Sheila E.	Jennifer Lopez	Cristina Saralegui	Tiger Woods
Gloria Estefan	Cheech Marin		

Library of Congress Cataloging-in-Publication Data
Wilson, Wayne, 1953-
    Shakira/Wayne Wilson.
        p. cm.—(A Real-life reader biography)
    Includes index.
    ISBN 1-58415-071-8
        1. Shakira—Juvenile literature. 2. Singers—Latin America—Biography—Juvenile literature. [1. Shakira. 2. Singers. 3. Hispanic Americans—Biography.] I. Title. II. Series.
    ML3930.S46 W55 2001
    782.42164'092—dc21
    [B]
                                                                  00-06766

ABOUT THE AUTHOR: Wayne Wilson was born and raised in Los Angeles. He received a Master of Arts in Education from the University of California, Los Angeles with a specialization in Sociology and Anthropology. For 16 years he was co-owner and president of a pioneering and innovative publishing company specializing in multicultural designs. In 2000, he completed interviews with influential Latino men throughout the country and wrote over 160 biographies for *Encuentros: Hombre A Hombre*, a comprehensive vocational education book to be published by the California Department of Education.

    Wilson has written four *Real-Life Reader Biography* books for children and young adults for Mitchell Lane Publishers. Wilson's short stories and essays have been published in commercial and literary magazines. He has finished his first original screenplay and was subsequently hired to work on another screenplay for a major Hollywood studio. He is also completing revisions on his first novel. Wilson lives in Venice Beach, California with his wife and daughter.

PHOTO CREDITS: cover: Archive Photos; pp. 4, 7,18, 22, 25 D. Baron Media Relations, Inc.; pp. 12, 23, 28 Archive Photos.

ACKNOWLEDGMENTS: The following story has been thoroughly researched, and to the best of our knowledge, represents a true story. While every possible effort has been made to ensure accuracy, the publisher will not assume liability for damages caused by inaccuracies in the data, and makes no warranty on the accuracy of the information contained herein. This story has not been authorized nor endorsed by Shakira.

Table of Contents

Chapter 1
A Woman Full of Grace

How many people by the age of 23 have sold millions of records, appeared on top commercial magazine covers, been named the national cultural ambassador of their native country, granted an audience with the Pope, interviewed by a winner of the Nobel Prize, acted in a soap opera, and endorsed major commercial products? Only one. And her name is Shakira.

Shakira lives in the South American country of Colombia. Her name, which means "woman full of grace" in Arabic, truly fits this gifted

Shakira comes from the South American country of Colombia.

young woman, who acts older than she really is. She is blessed with physical beauty, and she writes, dances, acts, plays the guitar, sings, and even produces her own songs. Her songs are very emotional and very inspirational to her fellow young Latin Americans. People often wonder how someone so young can write such deep, thoughtful music. "She is amazing," raves Gloria Estefan, one of her musical idols. And a writer for the *Los Angeles Times* says Shakira's eyes are "intense and intelligent."

When she was just thirteen, she was confident enough to sign a recording contract with Sony Music Colombia. She firmly explained to the executives that she did not want to become a "one-hit wonder" or change her singing style to be more commercial. Her persistence and efforts eventually resulted in the 1996 album *Pies Descalzos* ("Barefoot") that sold nearly four million copies. It launched her international career and when she went

Shakira sings, dances, acts, and even produces her own songs.

on tour she played to sold-out audiences worldwide.

When she sings, her voice is strong, passionate, and spirited — much like her dancing. As a result, her performances are electrifying. Yet she is able to reach out to her audience in a very warm and personal way. Her songs are so honest that you feel like she's letting you read passages from her diary. Shakira's poetic words talk about love, life, God, survival, and the way the world is today. They can be moody and solemn, but they also can be uplifting.

They are also the best way of getting to know Shakira, as she usually doesn't talk very much about her actual personal life.

"Her music is Shakira. It's real music," says her manager, the powerhouse producer Emilio Estefan. Estefan is the man behind the success of his wife Gloria Estefan. He produced Shakira's album *Dónde Están Los Ladrones* ("Where Are the Thieves?"), which sold nearly three million copies.

Shakira is passionate about her singing and dancing.

He believes that one day, Shakira will be as famous as other Latin American singers such as Ricky Martin or Selena.

Gloria Estefan was so impressed with Shakira's talents that she translated many of the songs from *Ladrones* for Shakira's first album in English, which also included some original songs. Gloria also helped Shakira with her English pronunciation and phrasing on many of the new songs. Shakira gained some valuable experience when she sang her rock ballad *Inevitable* in English on an episode of the Rosie O'Donnell Show with Gloria as the guest host.

Emilio Estefan constantly raves about Shakira. He says that she clearly knows who she is, what she wants, and how to get it. He adds she is "extremely well-adjusted, happy, and family-oriented." Although she may be a superstar performer, she chooses to live with her parents who she views as her "best friends." They often travel with her on the road.

Emilio and Gloria Estefan have helped her with her career in the United States.

Chapter 2
A Musical Prodigy

Shakira's father is Lebanese and her mother is Colombian.

The youngest of eight children, Shakira Isabel Mebarak Ripoll was born on February 2, 1977 in the town of Baranquilla, near Colombia's Caribbean coast. Her father is William Mebarak, a writer whose family is originally from Lebanon, a country in the Middle East. Her mother, Nidia Ripoll, is Colombian. Shakira's Lebanese and Colombian ancestry have had a large influence on her creativity. Her stage performances showcase her talent in Arabic dancing and her musical sound often features a hard-driving Latin American beat.

William and Nidia recognized their daughter's talents when she was a little girl. At an early age she began reading and writing. She scribbled poems to her parents, painted, sculpted, and sang her prayers at night. Her father introduced her to the deep thinkers of the world.

In an interview with *Seventeen* magazine, Shakira recalls how much he influenced her: "My father was a writer, and the image of him at his typewriter is very strong. I wanted to follow him." He introduced her to "la danza Arabe," a style of Middle Eastern dancing that she later put into her performances. She also learned to belly dance by the time she was five.

Shakira grew up with a fascination for music, particularly rock 'n' roll which she used to listen to with her friends. "Where I come from, people look for any excuse to move their hips," she laughs. By the time Shakira was eight, she realized that music and poetry were connected and wrote her first song.

Her father was a writer who also introduced her to Middle Eastern dancing.

Shakira can mesmerize an audience with her hip-swinging Arabic dancing. Here she is performing in Buenos Aires.

With her parents' support, she frequently entered singing contests in radio and television. When she was eleven, she won local and national talent shows as both a singer and guitarist. She was even kicked out of her school choir because her voice drowned out all of the other singers! But that didn't stop her. "Everyone thought our family was crazy, but my parents chased my dream by my side," she says proudly.

Record executives were so impressed by Shakira's musical ability that they signed her to a record deal in 1990 when she was only 13. They wanted their new singer to record more traditional music but Shakira had other intentions. She wasn't interested in exploring commercial music, the type of music that would sell a lot of albums. It was more important for her to record the music that was in her heart.

"To do Latin music would have been the easy way, but I like challenges," she said. She later told *Newsweek* magazine that she wanted to show the world that Latin American singers "don't just do ranchero and salsa. We can do good rock!"

In 1991, Shakira's first album, *Magia* ("Magic"), was released in Colombia when she was only 14 years old. It featured some of those songs that she had been writing since she was eight years old. It became popular in her country and her fellow Colombians began taking notice of their young

Shakira got her first record deal when she was only 13.

Shakira acted in a Colombian soap opera for three years.

musical genius. Shakira was invited to represent her country at the OTI Music Festival in Spain, but she couldn't compete because she had not yet reached the minimum age requirement.

Shakira followed up with a second album containing more original material entitled *Peligro* (Danger) which also did well. But at this point, Shakira took a break from music so that she could return to school and concentrate on her studies. After receiving her high school diploma, she decided to pursue a career in acting. She landed a role on the Colombian soap opera *El Oasis* from 1994 to 1997.

Chapter 3
International Superstar

But acting wasn't enough to satisfy the craving in Shakira's heart to create more music. Although she had developed a loyal fan base in Colombia with her first two albums, she wanted a breakthrough hit that would make her famous around the world. That opportunity came along in 1996 when she recorded the hugely successful album *Pies Descalzos* which combined rock, pop, and Latin rhythms.

The hit single *Estoy Aquí* shot to number one in eight countries and led to many other hit singles that included *Pienso En Ti* ("I think of you"), *Te*

But her heart is really in her music.

Necesito ("I need you"), and *Un Poco de Amor* ("A little bit of love"). The album was played a lot on Latin American radio stations and quickly rose to the top of the Latin Billboard charts. It led the music critic from a Miami newspaper to praise Shakira's "authentic sound that hadn't been heard before in Latin American pop." Other writers said she was one of the youngest and most promising Latin American stars of the decade.

So at the age of 19, Shakira was the top-selling female pop rocker in Latin America. Then she began touring around the world for almost two years performing her songs before sold-out crowds. Her parents weren't the only ones proud of their daughter's success. Her native country also swelled with pride and soon the president of Colombia made her an official goodwill ambassador. She shared that title with another famous Colombian, writer and Nobel Prize winner Gabriel Garciá Márquez. As an ambassador, she was

At the age of 19, Shakira became the top-selling female pop rocker in Latin America.

received by Pope John Paul II in the Vatican where she pleaded with him to try to help end Colombia's civil war, which had gone on for well over 30 years.

Because her career was really starting to take off, her longtime advisor, Jairo Martinez, decided it was time to find a producer who could help her reach her potential. So he approached Emilio Estefan, who quickly agreed to work with her. Their first collaboration in Estefan's Crescent Moon studios produced the album *Dónde Están Los Ladrones* which was released in September 1998 and sold over three million copies.

The title of the album refers to the theft of Shakira's luggage from the airport in Bogota, Columbia. The suitcases contained all of Shakira's sheet music, which had enough songs to fill up a compact disc. It was an unfortunate incident because she could not remember the songs and she didn't have any copies of them. So she had to come

Shakira was made an official goodwill ambas—sador for Colombia, and in this capacity, she got to meet Pope John Paul II.

up with all the material for the album from scratch.

"I decided on this title because it was a story that started with the luggage robbery, and two, because I had to find a way to justify dramatizing this incident," Shakira explains. "We're always looking for guilty ones to blame for our own inadequacies. We're all

thieves and have robbed in different ways. We carry some of the blame directly or indirectly. Including myself."

The album produced record-breaking sales and eventually went multi-platinum, which means that it sold several million copies. No one in the Spanish-speaking Latin American market had ever heard such a collection of music. It firmly established Shakira as a top performer and singer. *Dónde Están Los Ladrones* quickly climbed to the number one spot on Billboard's Latin 50. Shakira was named "Latin Female Artist of the Year" at the 1998 World Music Awards. She earned an award for "Best Female Album" on Billboard Latin Music Awards for *Dónde Están Los Ladrones*. Moreover, she was called the "Colombian Artist of the Millennium" by *TV y Novelas* magazine (1999).

Shakira's 1998 album was based on her experience losing all her luggage at the Bogata airport.

> ## *Chapter 4*
> # A Breakout Performance

With the success of *Ladrones,* Shakira became an international star and was chosen from among dozens of female Latin American singers to be on the cover of both *Time* and *Cosmopolitan* magazines' international editions. *Time* magazine also featured Shakira in an article that was called "Era of the Rocker." She made a Spanish-language commercial for Pepsi and has been featured in ads for Calvin Klein jeans.

Soon, MTV offered Shakira a chance to do an *Unplugged* show.

It wasn't long before MTV offered her an opportunity to do an *MTV Unplugged* show. Shakira helped to produce the show, and it featured

Shakira's solid back-up band, including Tim Mitchell on guitar and Luis Fernando Ochoa, who helps to write some of her songs. The concert showed off her incredible singing, Arabian dancing on the joyful *Ojos Así* ("Eyes Like That"), and a strong group of songs including *Octavo Día* ("The Eighth Day"), *Si Te Vas* ("If You Go"), *No Creo* ("I Don't Believe"), *Sombra de Ti* ("Shadows of You"), *Moscas en la Casa de Amor* ("Flies in the House of Love"), and *Ciega, Sordomuda* ("Blind, Deaf and Dumb").

Many people said it was her best work to date. The one-hour program was recorded live in front of an audience of 500 people in New York during the summer of 1999 in the Grand Ballroom of the Manhattan Center Studios. It was released in early 2000 to an American audience that was finally beginning to understand what all the fuss was about regarding this amazing Colombian singer and dancer.

It was recorded live in the Grand Ballroom of the Manhattan Center Studios.

Shakira won two Grammys at the first annual Latin Grammy Awards.

It became even more apparent when Shakira performed in the first annual Latin Grammy Awards on September 13, 2000, held in Los Angeles, California to celebrate the outstanding musical contributions of Latin American artists. The two-hour program, viewed in more than 120 countries, featured Shakira at her best. Dressed in a bright red pantsuit, she performed *Ojos Así* amidst dancers, images of water, and fiery special effects. She received a standing ovation as the audience cheered for more.

But the applause didn't end there because

Shakira won two Grammys. One was for Female Pop Vocal Performance (*Ojos Así*) and the other was for Female Rock Vocal Performance (*Octavo Día*). The awards seemed to prove what many people had been saying for a long time: No matter how great Shakira's recordings are, the excitement of seeing her in a live concert is even better.

Shakira with boyfriend Antonio de la Rua.

Chapter 5
A Crossover Success

There are several Latin American pop stars who have crossed over to the mainstream American market (Ricky Martin and Julio Iglesias), and rock stars who moved to the United States before starting a rock career (Carlos Santana, Ritchie Valens, and Los Lobos). But hardly any have been successful in Latin America first and then come to the United States. Shakira is on the verge of becoming the first big "Latin rock" crossover star, male or female.

The *Los Angeles Times* newspaper once asked Shakira where her songs come from. She answered that she

> **Shakira is trying to become a crossover success.**

receives inspiration from a place outside herself: "I definitely do not think I am in possession of my creative energy, or

that I have any control over it. I believe that if I write, it's because God wants me to do so. I always feel that when I write a song, a miracle has taken place."

Talent and inspiration have contributed a great deal to Shakira's success, but another ingredient has been her ability to remain focused on her goals. Shakira has embraced the long hours of work and discipline required to have a successful career. Considering how young she is, she has been remarkably successful in dealing with the pressures that are part of being a star. Nevertheless, she does admit that her songwriting serves as an "escape valve" and helps her cope with the problems of the world. "My entire body is a raw nerve," she says. "I write songs so I don't have to go to a psychiatrist."

Concentrating on her work has been beneficial to Shakira because unlike many artists searching for their roots, Shakira is comfortable in her own skin. She is earthy, centered, and knows who she is. She is one of those rare people who are unfazed by being in the spotlight. Moreover, Shakira Mebarak has been able to accept the different aspects of her personality. On the one hand, she is a passionate young woman who has a lot of experience with being in the world. On the other hand, she is comfortable with just hanging out at home with her family and going to

"I write songs so I won't have to go to a psychiatrist," says Shakira.

church regularly. She spends much of her free time reading two to three books a week.

A trailblazer in every way, Shakira has always followed her own path in life. She has been credited with creating her own image that changes constantly from flowing jet black hair to blond braids. You never know quite what to expect from Shakira. But she has very high expectations of herself and is a perfectionist when she records her music. She states that when she is in the process of developing an idea in the studio that she continuously questions herself. And she is never satisfied with the final product unless she finds a connection between herself and the music. She states, "We must be in unison, texture, quality, sound, taste, warmth, shape. A total embrace."

Furthermore, Shakira doesn't feel that you have to be tormented and suffering to write a song. She truly believes that you can be a positive and happy person, even if the material you

One really does not know what to expect during a perfor— mance by Shakira.

are composing is sad. In her estimation the key to honest expression is being able to observe what's going on in the world. You have to be able to collect emotions from people around you such as hate, love, joy, and passion and put them into words. She says that it is a lot like being a photographer: "I am inspired by reality in the same way a photographer is. A composer has to have the film loaded and open eyes. You have to let reality touch your senses. It is necessary to be vulnerable to everything and everyone."

Shakira hugs fans in Uruguay where she visited for several months in late 2000 to write songs for a new album.

Chapter 6
A Colombian Treasure

Praised as the voice of a new generation, Shakira is regarded by many people as one of the most exciting singers and songwriters to come out of Latin America in recent years. And though this young woman is already a major success with endless possibilities ahead, her most long-lasting and refreshing quality is her sincere love and respect for her people. She has not forsaken her roots. Shakira proudly uses her music and concerts as a way of communicating to an audience that is primarily young Latin Americans who view her as a positive role model. And

Young Latin Americans see Shakira as a positive role model.

unlike many performers who are only concerned about their record sales, Shakira truly appreciates the fact that her fans enjoy her so much. She is sincerely grateful for her success.

Her countrymen and countrywomen are her greatest motivation. She says that whenever she receives an award she thinks about her Colombian people because they make her proud and happy. When she accepted her first Latin Grammy Award, Shakira said "I want to dedicate this award to Colombia, which is going through some difficult times, but never forgot how to smile. This is for you, Colombia. *Para ti*, Colombia."

The *Los Angeles Times* asserts that the sales of Latin American music, including Latin rock, are growing at twice the overall rate of other types of music. Shakira has already sold over 10 million records and will be recognized as a major player in the Latin music surge throughout the world. In early 2001 she was in her studio in Uruguay

Shakira is proud and happy about her Colombian heritage.

where she was writing her first album of English material. As Sony Record Music Entertainment chief Tommy Mottola said, "Shakira is absolutely brilliant as an artist." But her fans know that she is also a generous and loving spirit who has redefined the boundaries of Latin American music. She is destined to play a major role in the revival of Latin pop and rock. And when this pioneer crosses over to a new level of popularity it's certain she will blaze a path for other Latin artists as well.

However, despite all the predictions for future success and the wonderful praise she has already received, Shakira recently told *Rolling Stone* magazine that "I don't promise I'm going to do a successful crossover. I just promise I'm going to do a great, great record." Anyone who has experienced Shakira's music knows this is a promise that this exceptionally talented artist will be sure to keep.

Shakira has already sold over 10 million records worldwide.

Chronology

- 1977, born to William Mebarak and Nidia Ripoll.
- 1990, signs record deal with Sony Music in Colombia at the age of 13.
- 1991, releases her first album, *Magia*.
- 1993, releases her second album, *Peligro*.
- 1994, lands role on soap opera *El Oasis*, which continues until 1997.
- 1996, releases *Pies Descalzos* which sells 3.6 million copies; is named the national cultural ambassador for Colombia; is received by the Pope in the Vatican.
- 1998, releases album *Dónde Están Los Ladrones* and it becomes multi-platinum by selling over 3 million copies to rate number one on Billboard's Latin 50; is named "Latin Female Artist of the Year" at the World Music Awards; earns award for "Best Female Album" on Billboard Latin Music Awards.
- 1999, named the "Colombian Artist of the Millennium" by *TV Y Novelas* magazine.
- 2000, releases *MTV Unplugged* album, performs *Ojos Así* on the 1st Annual Latin Grammy Awards and receives Grammys for Female Pop Vocal Performance and Female Rock Vocal Performance.
- 2001, wins Grammy for best Latin Pop Album with *MTV Unplugged*.

Index